CW00742055

# Purple Ronnie's Little Book of Pants

by Purple Ronnie

First published 2001 by Boxtree
an imprint of Macmillan Publishers Ltd
25 Eccleston Place London SW1W 9NF
Basingstoke and Oxford

www.macmillan.com

Associated companies throughout the world

ISBN 0 7522 7261 6



9 8 7 6 5 4 3 2

A CIP catalogue record for this book is available from the British Library

Text by Giles Andreae
Illustrations by Janet Cronin
Printed and Bound in Hong Kong

nice pants!

Part 1

# Men's Pants

a poem about
↓

# Men's Pants

Some men wear pants that
are sexy and tight
And some men wear pants
that are stringy
But some men go round with
no pants on at all
Cos they're just so in love
with their Thingy

chuck

i'm too sexy for my pants!

!

pants

thingy

# Willy Huggers

**What men think:** "I look like a sports god!"

**What girls think:** "Why is your thingy so knobbly?"

**Warning:** If you wear Willy Huggers for too long your voice goes all high and squeaky

**What men think**: "I like having it swinging around"

**What girls think**: "I can't tell how big your thingy is"

Be careful when you are wearing Posh Pants because your willy can come peering out of them without you noticing

# Grandad Pants

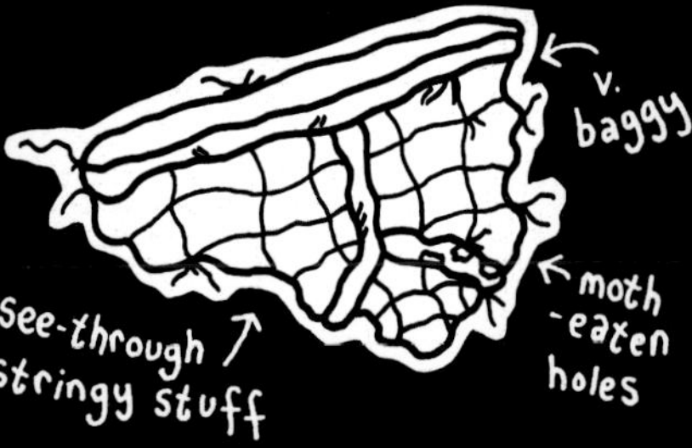

v. baggy

moth-eaten holes

See-through stringy stuff

**What men think:** "They'll be back in fashion one day my boy!"

**What girls think:** "Aah, how sweet!"

Men who wear grandad pants haven't even got the tiniest chance of pulling, but they're probably more interested in gardening anyway

# Trendy Pants

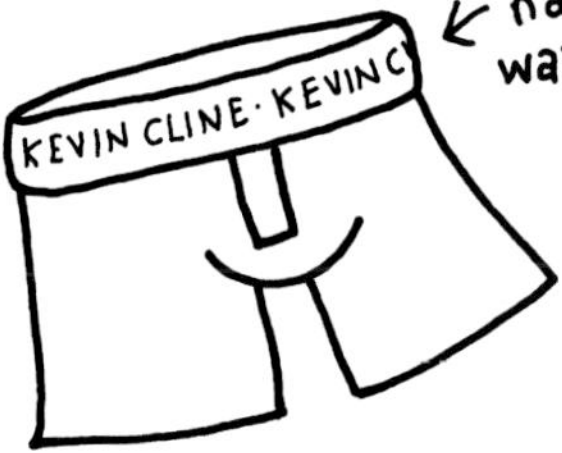

designer name on waistband

KEVIN CLINE · KEVIN C

botty-hugging shape

**What men think:** "Do I look like those blokes in the ads?"

**What girls think:** "Why don't you look like those blokes in the ads?"

Trendy pants are good at keeping your bits in place, but they do make them rather sweaty

# Y-Front Pants

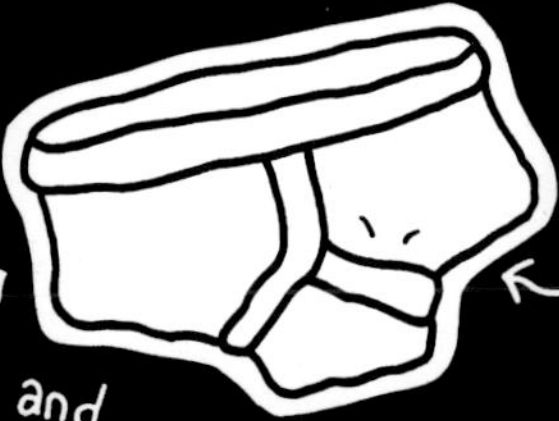

easy access willy hole

warm and cosy material

<u>What men think</u>: "Am I turning into my dad?"

<u>What girls think</u>: "I've got a headache!"

Y-Front pant wearers are always great lovers because they don't need sexy pants to make girls want them

# Girly Pants

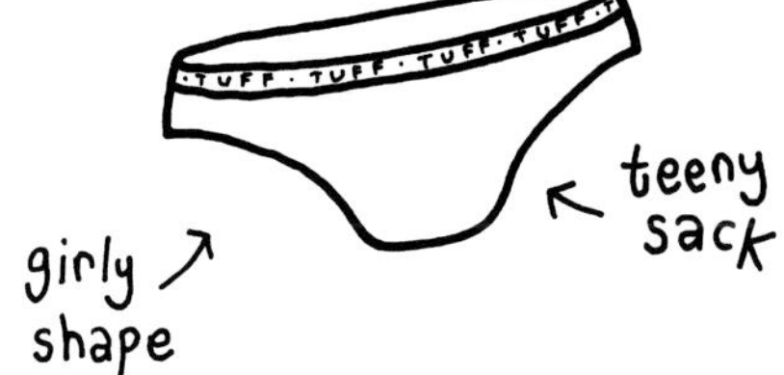


**What men think**: "These feel a bit slinky!"

**What girls think**: "Why are you wearing my pants?"

Because loads of men like wearing girls' pants, pant shops pretend that some girls' pants are men's pants, but they're not - they're girls' pants

# Posing Pants

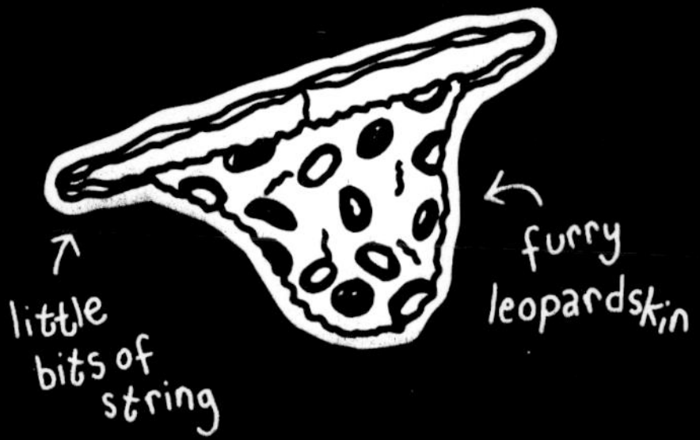

little bits of string

furry leopardskin

**What men think:** "Doesn't my packet look fab!"

**What girls think:** "Aagh! Scary!"

Posing Pants are worn by men with tiny willies who don't think they can pull without wrapping their bits up like a parcel

# Cod Pants

lace-up front
metal Studs
leather
bulge

**What men think:** "I wish I was born 400 years ago!"

**What girls think:** "You should be in prison"

Cod Pants were worn by men in medieval times. Once you had strapped them on you could stuff loads of vegetables down the front to make your packet look enormous

hi girls!

Squash

# Space Pants

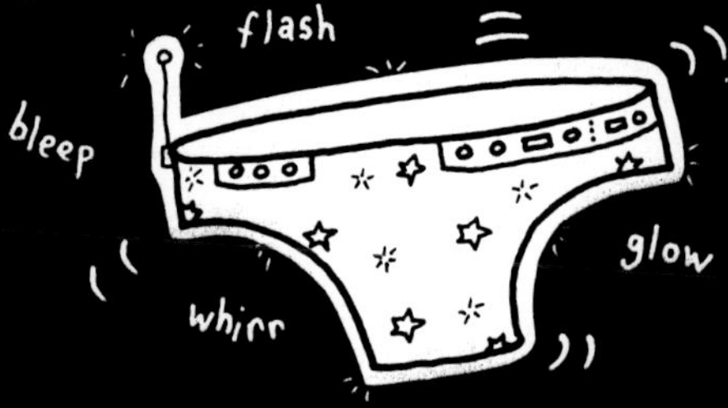

flash

bleep

glow

whirr

What men think: "At last, the ultimate gadget!"

What girls think "Men are weird!"

In the future, Space Pants will be able to do anything you want them to

# Part 2

# Girls' Pants

rummage

a poem about

# Girls' Pants

Some girls wear huge comfy
pants
That help them to relax
But others wear small
stringy ones
That go right up their
cracks

girls in
their pants

ooh!

tug

squeeze

comfy

stringy

# Up-Yer-Bum Pants

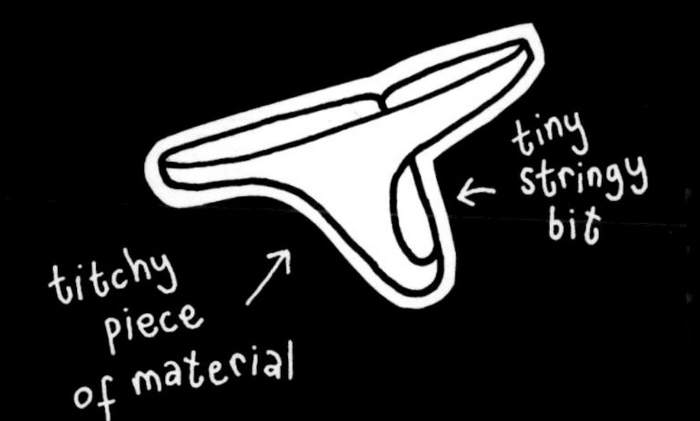


**What girls think:** "No one can see if I'm wearing any pants!"

**What men think:** "Hey! No pants!"

Up-Yer-Bum Pants are usually only worn by skinny people. Lardy bottoms do not look good in Up-Yer-Bums

# Granny Pants

**What girls think:** "I look like the star of an old soppy movie!"

**What men think:** "Aaagh! You look like my gran!"

People who wear Granny Pants are usually very shy about showing their bottoms

# Pulling Pants

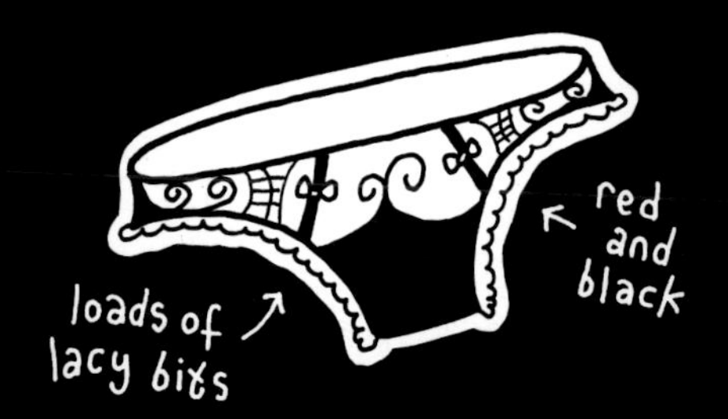


**What girls think:** "I know they're tarty but they work every time!"

**What men think:** "Get 'em off!"

Pulling Pants were invented to make men's trousers explode

# Squashing Pants

**What girls think:** "Ooh look, I'm 2 sizes smaller!"

**What men think:** "What are those bulgy bits at the top of your pants?"

Squashing Pants were invented to make your tummy look smaller. Do not wear them for too long or you might stop breathing

# Slinky Pants

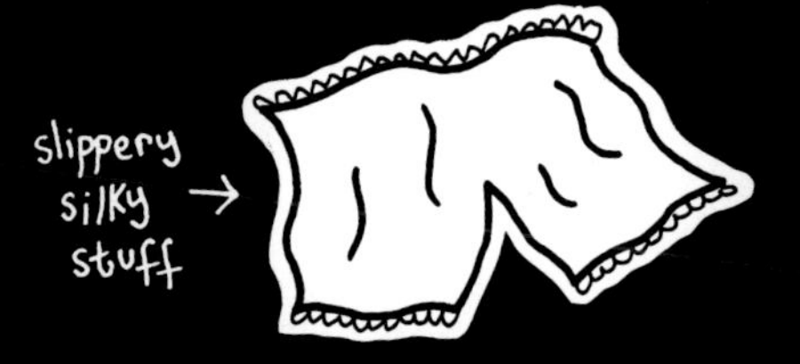


**What girls think:** "Ooh... these are nice and breezy!"

**What men think:** "Classy bird!"

The only point of wearing slinky pants is for other people to see them

bonjour!

pout

Slinky Pants are usually only given as presents by boyfriends

# Work Pants

used to be stretchy

hole

greyish colour

no frilly bits

**What girls think:** "No one will see them so it doesn't matter"

**What men think:** "Yuck!"

Work Pants are what you wear when you can't be bothered to find anything else

What girls think: "What a great invention!"

What men think: "What are they for?"

Spray-On Pants are best under really tight dresses. Never let a boy try on your Spray-Ons or they will burst

# Love Pants

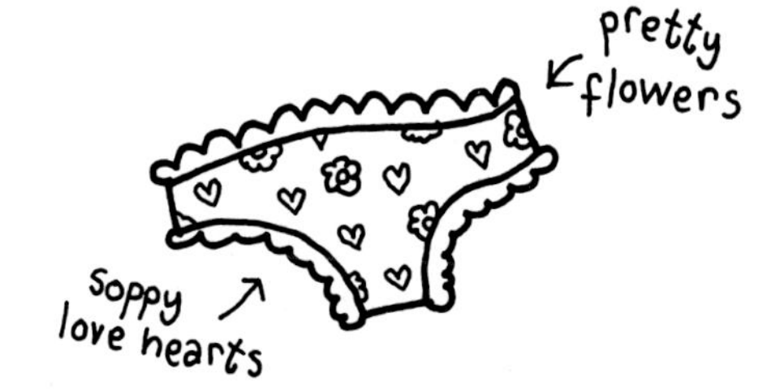


**What girls think:** "I feel all pretty and girly!"

**What men think:** "I wonder if she'll ever let me Do It with her?"

Love Pants are worn by people who like to cuddle a lot

# Mummy Pants

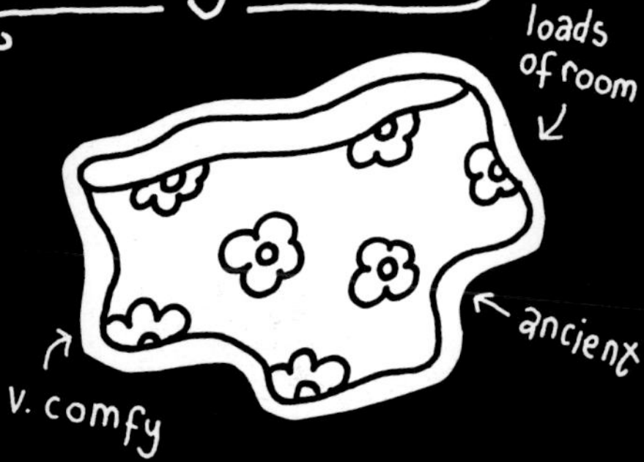

loads of room

ancient

v. comfy

**What girls think:** "Do I know him well enough to wear these?"

**What men think:** "I wonder what's on telly?"

Mummy Pants should only be worn if you have been Doing It with the same person for at least 10 years

hooray!